EDGE BOOKS

BICYCLE STUNT RIDING

by Russ Spencer

Content Adviser: James Ayres,
Associate Editor, Transworld BMX
magazine, Tustin, California

WITHDRAWN

Published in the United States of America by The Child's World®
PO Box 326 • Chanhassen, MN 55317-0326 • 800-599-READ • www.childsworld.com

Acknowledgments

The Child's World®: Mary Berendes, Publishing Director

Editorial Directions, Inc.: E. Russell Primm, Editorial Director; Melissa McDaniel, Line Editor; Matt Messbarger, Project Editor and Editorial Assistant; Susan Hindman, Copy Editor; Susan Ashley, Proofreader; Terry Johnson, Olivia Nellums, Katharine Trickle, and Julie Zaveloff, Fact Checkers; Tim Griffin/IndexServ, Indexer; James Buckley Jr. and James Gigliotti, Photo Researchers and Selectors

Editorial and photo research services provided by Shoreline Publishing Group LLC, Santa Barbara, California

The Design Lab: Kathleen Petelinsek, Art Direction and Design; Kari Thornborough, Art Production

Photos

Cover: image 100/Punchstock; Chase Jarvis/Corbis: 11; Duomo/Corbis: 23; Al Fuchs/ NewSportCorbis: 26; Steve Granitz/WireImage: 29; Jason Merritt/WireImage: 24; Kelly-Mooney/Corbis: 20; Pete Saloutos/Corbis: 17; William Sallaz/Duomo/Corbis: 16; Sports Gallery/Al Messerschmidt: 5, 6, 8, 9, 12, 14, 19, 21, 22, 27, 28; Chris Trotman/Corbis: 25.

Library of Congress Cataloging-in-Publication Data

Spencer, Russ.
  Bicycle stunt riding / by Russ Spencer.
    v. cm. — (Kids' guides)
  Includes bibliographical references and index.
  Contents: History of a hybrid—Gears and events—Let the good times roll—The bicycle big time.
  ISBN 1-59296-207-6 (Library bound : alk. paper) 1. Bicycle motocross—Juvenile literature.
  2. Stunt cycling—Juvenile literature. [1. Bicycle motocross. 2. Stunt cycling.] I. Title. II. Series.
  GV1049.3.S64 2005
  796.6—dc22   2003027366

CONTENTS

HUMANS AND MACHINES

The bicycle was built for transportation.

Long before the automobile came along, the bike gave people a way to get from here to there quickly. The first bicycles, created in the 1800s, had enormous front wheels, sometimes as large as 6 feet (2 meters) tall. The pedals were on the front tires instead of the back. The wheels were made out of metal, which made for a bumpy and uncomfortable ride.

As the bicycle evolved, it became sleeker, lighter, and faster. It no longer had those huge front wheels. New rubber tires created a smooth ride. Still, the bike was basically just a way for kids and adults to get to school, or shopping, or work. Some special bikes were used for racing, but not by a large number of people.

This dull way of thinking about bikes lasted until the 1980s. Then, suddenly, some bicycles underwent a complete reinvention. With a few modifications, they became stunt machines. Bikes have now followed skateboards, surfboards, and snowboards into the exciting world of extreme sports. And that means the bike is now a means of expression. These days, getting from here to there on a bike involves getting there in a **rad** way.

Stunt bicycle riding is a highly individualistic sport. It's a way for you to do your own thing. But a lot of people also ride together. All over the world, there are stunt riding or "freestyle" bicycle groups. Most are comprised of a bunch of friends who like to ride together. Kids get together on the weekends or after school to work on stunts, take pictures of each other, or make their own videos. There are hundreds of stunt riding Web sites, some of them official. Most of them, though, are made by kids **stoked** on the sport.

There are now five basic kinds of stunt riding (which will be defined in the next chapter): dirt jumping, **flatland,** street, **park riding,** and vert. Flatland is fairly safe, but dirt jumping, street riding, park riding, and vert all involve high speeds and riders who get airborne. All of these kinds of riding require practice, skill, and a lot of courage.

Performing tricks on a bike is in some ways more complex than skating, surfing, or snowboarding. That's because

Riding on air? Bicycle stunt riders can do just about anything with their bikes. For a few precious seconds, they can even take flight!

Balancing on one wheel is a key freestyle skill.

there are so many ways to ride a stunt bike. Some stunt riders even do back flips on them. Stunt bikes are altered so that riders can stand on the front or back axles. Riders often use the bicycle as if it were a dance partner, spinning it around their bodies and climbing over it as they ride. In stunt riding, balance and precision are as important as speed and height.

It is this blend of delicacy and danger that has made stunt riding a fast-growing sport. Bicycle stunt, or freestyle, is quickly becoming the biggest deal in the BMX, or bicycle motocross, cycling scene. Fewer than 10 bike companies were represented in the 1995 X Games. By 1999, there were close to 20, and since then that number has continued to grow at an amazing rate. There are now freestyle riders throughout Asia, Europe, and South America.

Read on (and ride on!) to find out more about this hot new sport.

CHAPTER one

HISTORY OF A HYBRID

Bicycle stunt riding is a hybrid—

its moves and tricks are adapted from many other sports.

Freestyle riding's roots are tied most closely to motocross

racing, which became popular in the 1960s. Motocross races

feature big fields of motorcycle riders racing around dirt

courses. Along the way, the riders make big jumps and spin

through grinding, banked curves. It is a loud and dirty sport,

but very exciting to watch.

In California, some innovative kids, too young to ride

motorcycles, began riding their bikes in empty fields and lots.

They were imitating motocross riders. Like most great sports,

these kids invented it out of nothing. No one told them to do it.

They just started doing it, all on their own.

At the time, most of these kids rode Schwinn Stingrays,

popular bikes that their parents had bought them to ride to

school. These weren't the strongest bikes of all time. But the

kids adapted the bikes, beefing them up to make them stronger

and faster.

By the time the 1970s rolled around, bike riders had

a new sport, all their own. It was called bicycle motocross,

or BMX. At first, BMX was just like motocross. Riders took

their bikes around a track and caught air when they went

BMX racers such as this one were the forerunners, or "fore-riders," of today's stunt bikers.

over **whoop-de-dos.** They wore motorcycle helmets, body padding, and gloves.

As time went on, though, BMX riders began to pick up moves from skateboarders. At first, these tricks involved fancy things the riders did after launching into a jump. After a while, riders began doing tricks on the street and in freestyle events, just like skaters. They didn't need dirt tracks anymore.

While BMX continues, stunt riding has become its own, completely different type of bike riding. Freestyle riders and BMX racers may wear the same or similar protective gear, but unlike BMX, freestyle riding isn't a race. Freestyle riding has nothing to do with speed. It is an exhibition of skill and talent.

In just 10 years, bike riders had invented two entirely new sports. Freestyle riders continued to refine and expand their sport, and in 1983, bicycle companies called Haro and Mongoose

Unlike stunt-bike models, some BMX bikes have larger wheels with more rugged tread.

began making freestyle bikes that you could buy in stores. The bikes had stronger frames than most bikes, which allowed riders to do punishing tricks without breaking their bikes.

The following year, the first competitions were held, mostly in California skate parks. By 1985, sponsors were putting money into prizes. Competitions expanded throughout the country. After freestyle riding was included in the 1995 X Games, it became hugely popular.

Eventually, five different types of events were developed for the sport:

- Dirt jumping: cyclists do tricks after getting air off of dirt mounds.
- Flatland: cyclists do tricks while rolling slowly over a flat parking lot or platform.
- Street: stunts are performed while the cyclists ride over obstacles found in the street, such as curbs, planters, and railings.
- Vert: bike riders do amazing tricks while getting incredible air on a vertical **half-pipe,** such as the kind used in skateboarding.
- Park riding: riders perform a blend of vert, flatland, and street maneuvers in a park that includes a variety of ramps and obstacles.

BMX ROLLS ON

Even as stunt riding has taken off, BMX is still a popular sport. Many towns have BMX tracks. Often they were created by the parents of young riders. Local and national competitions are held for boys and girls of all ages.

A typical BMX race is a sprint—one lap around a track that is usually about 1,000 feet (300 m) long. But those thousand feet might include washboard bumps that rattle your teeth (right), whoop-de-do jumps that send you flying, and high, banked curves.

At BMX tracks, racers are put into a "moto," or group of kids the same age and all at about the same skill level. Riders wear helmets and gloves and ride padded bikes. After the racers line up, a metal gate drops and all the riders start pedaling down the start hill. The first one around the track to the finish line wins. It's fast, furious, dirt-churning action and another great way to use your bike.

Stunt freestyle bikes are smaller than mountain bikes and road racing bikes. The frames are usually heavier and less complicated. The wheels are 20 inches (51 centimeters) in diameter, as much as a foot smaller than "normal" bikes. This makes it easy for a rider to climb all over the bike while performing tricks.

At the same time, these bikes have to be strong. They have to be stronger than the bike you take to school. They even have to be stronger than most BMX bikes. The strongest and heaviest of all stunt bikes are those used to ride vert on. They

This close up shows how small the stunt bike frames are. Note the lack of gears on this bike.

need to be strong because the riders sometimes plunge back to the half-pipe from more than 10 feet (3 m) in the air.

The core of all stunt bikes is the frame, the part that holds the wheels, the seat, the handlebars, and the pedals together. Even stunt bike frames are hybrid—they are made of chromoly, a very strong mix of two metals called chromium and molybdenum.

Frames come in different sizes. If you are under 5 feet, 4 inches (163 cm) tall, you'll want a frame size of 18.5 to 19.5 inches (47 to 49.5 cm) top tube length. Frame sizes go all the way up to 22 inches (56 cm), but these are for people more than 6 feet (2 m) tall. Good bike shops will help you choose the right frame.

Almost all stunt riders add **pegs** to their axles. The pegs stick straight out from the middle of each wheel. The rider balances on the pegs while doing tricks.

A variety of different high-strength rims are also available. Almost all freestyle riders prefer 20-inch (51-cm) rims. Normal bicycles have 26-inch (66-cm) rims. Dirt jumping riders prefer to put tires with a heavy tread on the rims. The heavy tread allows them to get a better grip on the dirt. Other stunt riders tend to use tires with less tread so that their ride is faster and smoother.

The rider's feet rest on special pedals. These pedals have rough studs built into their surface, to help keep the rider's feet from slipping off.

The handlebars of a stunt bike stick straight up from the bike so that they can spin around with- out hitting the bike or the rider. They come with heavy rubber handgrips and have hand brakes at the end of each bar.

Freestyle riders rely on a lot of safety equipment. The more intense their riding is, the more safety equipment they wear, including pads and gloves. Riders always wear helmets, and they can choose from a variety of helmets,

Helmets, elbow and kneepads, and special bike gloves are all necessary safety equipment for riders.

BRAKES: GRIPS, CABLES, AND DETANGLERS

Some say brakes are the most important piece of equipment on a stunt bike. On regular small bikes, the brakes are on the pedals. Stunt bike brakes, however, are on the handlebars, with one brake at each handgrip. When riders balance on one tire, they use the brakes to stop the tire from rolling. For a lot of stunt tricks, it's very important to be able to stop the front and back tires individually.

The brakes have cables that run from the handgrips to the tires. The amazing thing about stunt bike brakes is that they work even when the handlebars spin all the way around. Some bikes come with cables that are so long the handlebars spin underneath them. But other bikes have special devices called detanglers. The brake cables enter the detangler, and no matter which way they come in or out, they still work. Detanglers enable the bike rider to spin the handlebars all the way around without tangling the brake cables.

As cool as these brake systems are, some top riders, including Mat Hoffman (see page 29), don't use any brakes at all. They prefer to keep their bikes as simple as possible.

including full-face motocross helmets, skate helmets, and typical bike helmets.

Putting a good freestyle bike together is expensive, costing $200 to more than $1,000. Don't expect to have a top-of-the-line stunt bike overnight. Typically, a beginning rider will start doing tricks on the bike he already owns. As interest in the sport deepens, a rider can slowly buy better equipment.

There are so many types of stunt

Learning about your bike by just riding around in the street is the best way to begin practicing.

riding, it may be hard to know where to begin. Are you into speed and thrills? Then you may want to do dirt riding and jumps. Are you more into delicate moves? Then try out some flatland tricks. For many, what they choose depends on where they live and what kind of landscape is available to ride on.

The first place to begin trying tricks is the playground or an empty parking lot. Start to practice anywhere you can ride without getting in anyone's way. As you get better on your bike, begin to try small jumps, even if they are just off curbs or on small ramps. As you get better, your own interests will begin to guide you into the kind of riding you want to do.

Also, as you improve, you will want to begin adding stunt gear to your bike, such as special

Taking small jumps over ramps or off of curbs helps you get a feel for "getting air."

brakes and pegs. The biggest thing to remember is this: stunt riding is very difficult. Tricks take a lot of discipline and patience to learn. Some tricks can take years to perfect.

Flatland riding is like a dance. A rider can make her bike ride on one wheel. She can pop a **wheelie** and spin the handlebars. Riders climb all over their bikes and hop on their back tires as if they were pogo sticks. A rider might do an **endo** and a **bunny hop.** Eventually, riders are able to create a flowing series of tricks that take the skill of a ballet dancer and the courage of a motorcycle racer.

The next move for many freestyle riders is to do street stunts. Street riders use obstacles found on city sidewalks and streets to perform tricks. They hop onto benches, jump over railings, and rattle down staircases. Using the wheel pegs, they slide along rails and balance on the edge of low walls. Street riding is a combination of creativity and bike skills.

In park riding competitions, a special arena is set up to look like a street scene. Riders zoom up ramps, fly over jumps, and slide along rails. While in the air, they spin and flip their bikes. Competitors are judged on their creativity and style. It is not unusual to see a rider crash while trying a tough new trick. But they usually pop up and start riding again right away.

One of the most exciting forms of stunt riding is vert, where riders cruise back and forth on a half-pipe. After dropping into the U, riders head straight down the steep side of the

In park competitions, riders go on and over man-made obstacles; here a rider does a trick called an ice pick on a ramp edge.

half-pipe. Gathering speed, they race up the other side and fly into the air.

Once airborne, they do flips, spins, and twists before landing (they hope) back on the ramp. Vert riders can fly more than 10 feet (3 m) above the half-pipe, which can be 20 feet (6.1 m) tall. When vert riders really fly, it's called "getting big air." The higher they fly, the longer they have to flip, twist, and spin. Some of the best-known tricks are:

BEGINNING AT THE ENDO

One of the most basic of all freestyle tricks is the endo. Endo is short for "end-over." In other words, your bike's back end rises up over its front end. The trick is pretty easy, and it will get you on your way. When you learn it, you'll begin to understand your bike as a trick machine.

To do an endo, you ride slowly into a curb. When your front tire hits the curb, lean forward. Using the momentum of the bike, pull your body up and over the handlebars just a little and lift the back wheel up in the air.

You can also do an endo by simply riding along and then hitting your front brakes. When the tire locks, lean forward. Push the back wheel off the ground. When you've done this a few times, begin to try to balance on the front tire. Your stunt riding skills have just started with the endo.

- 360: the rider and the bike spin around in a complete circle. The trick gets its name from the 360 degrees it takes to make a full circle.
- Tailwhip: after getting big air, the rider kicks his feet off the pedals and spins the bike underneath him, while holding onto the handlebars.
- Barspin: the rider spins the handlebars, letting them twirl one full rotation before catching them and landing.

THE BICYCLE BIG TIME

Freestyle riding has become popular

because you don't need an ocean or a snow-covered mountain to stage an event. All you need is a parking lot or a half-pipe. And almost every kid has a bike.

Vert riding has become one of the most popular forms of freestyle riding. That's because vert riders put on a big show,

The most spectacular bicycle stunt tricks are performed on the half-pipe. Here a rider soars above one side of the pipe.

Once in the air, riders can do tricks, such as taking their feet off the pedals.

often with lights, loud music, and four or five guys riding one right after the other. This style of riding has become part of the wave of extreme sports. Sometimes stunt riders will perform on the same vert pipe as skateboarders, while hot young rock bands play nearby.

Vert doubles, with two riders performing on the same vert pipe, is also getting more popular. That's because it's completely dazzling. Two guys play off each other's skills in a double dose of extreme talent.

Stunt riding is now popular all over the world. This is because events such as the X Games and the Gravity Games are shown on television. At the annual MTV Sports and Music Festival, famous stunt riding stars such as Mat Hoffman, Dave Mirra, and Chad Kagy are treated like rock stars. These riders tour all over the world like other celebrities. They sign autographs and have their own Web sites.

Superstar Dave Mirra drops in, gaining speed to perform another spectacular, high-flying trick.

Freestyle riding has no single governing body, but many competitive events are run by the Hoffman Sports Association, which was started by Mat Hoffman's Hoffman Promotions. And the number of X Games competitions is growing. Starting in 1998, riders began competing in the Asian X Games and, later, the Latin X Games in Brazil and the Europe X Games.

Riders from foreign countries are beginning to come to the United States to compete. This makes the stunt riding competition very fierce. As a result, tricks are becoming more and more amazing.

Huge crowds at the X Games watch stunt bike riders and other extreme sports stars.

In flatland, it's just you and your bike in a ballet of wheels and spokes.

Vert is one of the star events at the X Games, but flatland events are also popular. Riders consider flatland events very "technical." This means that they are more about technique than soaring in the air. A flatland rider treats his bike like an obstacle, figuring out more and more difficult ways to balance on it and do tricks on it. Judges are increasingly interested not

X Games "street" competition sends riders over obstacles similar to those found on city streets.

only in the difficulty of the trick but also in the originality of the performance.

At the X Games, riders perform on street-style obstacle courses as well. The riders pull off tricks that blend flatland

The dirt-jump competition combines the sport's BMX roots with aerial tricks.

with vert, including tricks with funny names such as the "one-footed X-up backflip," the "superman tailwhip," and the "jump-over ice pick." The X Games also include dirt events where riders continue to perform just as they did in the early days of stunt riding, doing tricks when they go over jumps.

Because stunt bike riding is so popular, more and more stunt bike companies have opened. They have been giving professional riders **sponsorships.** These bike companies are also creating better equipment for amateurs. That brings up the level of skill in parks and parking lots all over the country. The gap between pro riders and up-and-coming riders is getting narrower all the time.

Keep riding, and someday maybe you'll get to name your own trick!

Look, mom, no hands! Only the most expert free-style riders can attempt tricks such as this one.

THE CONDOR FLIES HIGH

Mat Hoffman is nicknamed the Condor because when he takes off from a vert pipe, he looks like he's flying. He holds the record for "biggest air"—he once flew higher than a five-story building.

Hoffman is the most successful stunt bike rider ever. He has won 10 world championships in 10 years, and in the 2002 X Games, he pulled off the world's first no-handed 900. In this trick, he launched himself off the vert pipe and spun around in the air almost three times without having his hands on the bike. Incredible.

Mat also runs Hoffman Bikes and has a best-selling stunt bike video game.

But he has paid a price for his success. In flying higher, he has also slammed harder. He's broken 45 bones altogether. He has had 14 operations to fix injuries he got from falls. He's taken so much punishment, he has artificial **ligaments** in his knee. That's extreme, dude.

GLOSSARY

bunny hop—A trick in which the rider pops the bike off the ground without going over any ramps or obstacles.

endo—A simple trick in which the rider balances on the front wheel.

flatland—A type of riding in which the rider performs tricks in a flat, open area with no obstacles.

half-pipe—A ramp that looks like a giant letter U.

hybrid—Something made up of two or more things.

ligaments—Tough bands of tissue that connect bones and hold some organs in place.

park riding—A type of riding in which the rider does tricks over a group of man-made obstacles.

pegs—Round metal pieces that attach to the outside of the axles of a stunt bike; riders stand on the pegs during certain tricks.

rad—Short for *radical*; impressive, extreme.

sponsorships—Deals usually given to an athlete or celebrity in which they endorse a certain product in exchange for money.

stoked—Feeling good, enthusiastic, and happy about something.

wheelie—A trick in which a bike rider pops or pulls one wheel off the ground and keeps riding or doing other tricks.

whoop-de-dos—A series of small humps or large bumps on a BMX bike-racing course.

FIND OUT MORE

On the Web

Visit our home page for lots of links about stunt bicycle riding:
http://www.childsworld.com/links.html

NOTE TO PARENTS, TEACHERS, AND LIBRARIANS: We routinely check our Web links to make sure they're safe, active sites—so encourage your readers to check them out!

Books (Nonfiction)

Eck, Kristin. *Bicycle Stunt Riding: Check It Out!* New York: PowerKids Press, 2001.

Hayhurst, Chris. *Bicycle Stunt Riding!* New York: Rosen Central, 2000.

Nelson, Julie. *BMX Racing and Freestyle.* Austin, Tex.: Steadwell Books, 2002.

Books (Fiction)

Christopher, Matt. *Dirt Bike Runaway.* Boston: Little, Brown & Company, 1983.

Christopher, Matt, and Barry Bomzer (illustrator). *Dirt Bike Racer.* Boston: Little, Brown & Company, 1979.

Sachar, Louis, and Amy Wummer (illustrator). *Marvin Redpost: Super Fast, Out of Control!* New York: Random House, 2000.

INDEX

About the Author

Russ Spencer is a Southern California writer, filmmaker, and surfer. His articles have appeared in publications such as *Outside*, the *Surfer's Journal*, the *New York Times* Sunday magazine, *Utne Magazine*, and the *Los Angeles Times*.